Governance Pitfalls

DANGER
When Boards
Become Clubs

S. L. Austin PhD

This book is dedicated to all the talented men and women who volunteer their considerable skills and expertise to serve the boards that govern the diverse enterprises across our nation.

Table Of Contents

Prologue

This is a book about board dynamics. It is not a *how–to* book but a *thinking* book.

By means of a fictional story, you will be led through the potential pitfalls awaiting you as a member of a board of directors *if* you fail to do your due diligence. A researcher and a detective team together to uncover the elements that led to the demise of a once fully functioning board. The nebulous Agency, which could be any oversight entity, adds a touch of mystery to the scenario that unfolds.

Remember, the purpose of this book is to elicit thought. At strategic points in the storyline, you will be asked what you are thinking and prompted to focus your thoughts on specific issues. Every time, ask yourself if you and/or your colleagues have fallen or could fall into any of the traps that have been identified. If you answer yes to either of these questions, you know you have work to do with respect to the governance of your board. Good luck!

Cast Of Characters

The Researcher or Search – PhD in governance focusing on board governance issues and board development

The Detective or Gov – member of a law enforcement agency specializing in corporate and white-collar fraud

◆ ◆ ◆

Mr. Smythe – former president of the Organization

Mr. Prim – current president of the Organization

Mr. Wilson – former chair of the board of the Organization

Ms Fall – followed Wilson as board chair while Smythe was still president

Mrs. Sackmaster – current board chair

Ms Vinn – fired vice president

Mr. Bentley – retired vice president

Mr. Dung – current vice president

◆◆◆

The Agency – an oversight entity. Lack of specification allows you to interpret the Agency as pertinent to your circumstances. Among others, it could be a securities commission, an exchange, a parent company, or a level of government.

The Organization – the company or institution currently under scrutiny by the Agency. Lack of specification allows you to determine the type of organization that best fits your circumstances.

The Present

"No one is going to believe this," the Detective mumbled to himself as he idly flicked the data stick between his fingers. Staring blankly into space, he failed to notice the figure approaching from behind.

"Hey, Gov, deep in thought, I see."

Lifting his head, he saw the glint of amusement in her eyes, seeming almost to mock his dark thoughts. "Do you really think anyone is going to take us seriously? Just look at this stuff!" He thrust the data stick in her direction. "Maybe I should start my report with 'Once upon a time'."

Sympathetic, she shrugged her shoulders. "I've had those same thoughts more times than I can say. In all my years of research, this one takes the cake. It sounds more like a soap opera, doesn't it?"

"And I thought this was going to be a lark – nice folks doing nice work to help out companies that affect their communities." He hesitated, lowering his voice. "These people are absolutely vicious and conniving. And they do it under the guise of sweet community service. And for what? A little power and control that lasts for . . . how long?" He shook his head in exasperation and sighed heavily. "Makes corporate fraud appear almost sane. At least there I know who the bad guys are."

Nodding in affirmation, she perched on the edge of his desk. "Think of it this way: we file our report, answer any questions, and walk away, never to see those people again, thank goodness. I don't think I can last much longer without taking them to task myself." Her eyes brightened. "Look on the positive side; at least we're finally free to get back to our real lives."

Grinning up at his partner, he chuckled softly. "Search, do you remember the first time we met? You were spitting mad."

She laughed. "You weren't exactly Mr. Happy yourself."

The Past

She kicked open the already ajar office door and slammed a stack of files down on the desk, giving it a kick, too, for good measure. "This had better be good, that's all that I can say," she muttered. On the plane, she had been in more of a controlled burn, but the anger was seething through her now. "How could they!" A few choice expletives emerged, making her feel a little better.

The jet lag had gotten the better of her, she rationalized. At least she was alone now and could try to get a grip. What could be important enough to drag her halfway around the world? "Those self-serving, insensitive . . ." A few more well-placed expletives were needed, and maybe then she could start thinking more clearly. Suddenly, she heard a rustling sound to her left and could feel her face begin to flush.

With growing embarrassment, she stammered, "Don't tell me I've walked into the wrong office!" Without looking up, she hastily tried to collect the pile of folders to make a rapid exit. "I'm *so* sorry."

"Oh, I don't think you have the wrong office." The calm, male voice startled her.

Her head snapped up, and she turned in the direction of the voice. "What? What do you mean?" She was tired and had no desire to play games.

"You're the Researcher, right?"

She scowled in reply.

"I'm your new partner, and from the sound of things, we both feel the same way about this assignment."

"Partner? No one said anything about a partner. I work alone!"

"Just got in, didn't you?" He casually tossed wads of paper into a trash can across the room. "More good news: apparently there's a briefing in a few minutes."

"Of all the nerve, those – " This time she caught herself before the expletives came out. Instead, she grabbed a couple of folders and slammed them repeatedly on the desk.

The look of exasperation on her face made him want to chuckle, but he thought it best to hold it back for the time being. Just a short while before, he had felt the same way. He'd had the time to settle down. Besides, he only had to fly across the country. She, on the other hand, had flown halfway around the world.

"I was already in the country, so I got here faster. Been here for a few hours. Things seem real mysterious, so thought I'd start filling in the blanks. By the way, I'm the Detective."

She frowned. "Detective? Have they gone mad? Why ever would I need a detective?" She abruptly stopped her ranting and looked at him suspiciously. "There's more to this than just a quick research project, isn't there?"

"Uh huh" came his confident reply. "The Agency must have screwed up one way or the other."

"Terrific," she replied sarcastically while slumping into the vacant chair. Sighing heavily she asked, "Have you any idea what's going on?"

"Well, this is what I've been able to piece together so far . . ."

The Assignment

Well, that was not what she had expected at all. Fortunately, the Detective had done some reconnaissance prior to her arrival. If he hadn't, she would have felt like a complete idiot at the briefing.

"Thank you," she said apologetically, trying to force a smile. "I know we didn't get off to a very good start. That was all my fault." She took a long look at the Detective. He was tall and well-built with short, chestnut hair and brown eyes that had a strange depth to them. She estimated that he was near her age, somewhere in his early forties. For someone who had been pulled from his work with no warning, he had a calmness about him that she liked immediately.

"I was just so angry at being called back here that I wasn't thinking very clearly. At least now I know why they called *me* specifically . . . though it doesn't make me any happier." From her perch on the edge of her desk, she looked down at the floor and gave a heavy sigh.

He gave her a moment to mull over their situation, during which he noticed how attractive she was. She wore a navy, striped pant suit that flattered her trim figure. Light-brown curls fell around her shoulders. He already liked her feisty demeanor. *This assignment might not be so bad after all*, he thought.

For the first time since her arrival, the Researcher looked around their office. There were two old-style wood desks at an angle from one another and wooden office chairs that looked like they belonged in a 1950s movie. "They sure did put us in an old office. Look at this wood paneling." She ran her hand softly over the smooth, dark surface. "It's quite lovely."

"Looks like they wanted to hide us from the rest of the staff. We're kinda buried in the bowels of this huge building. I, for one, like the privacy."

"I do too. And it's nice to see they have provided an excellent array of technology for our use."

Curiosity got the best of him. "By the way, exactly what were you doing overseas? Seems like a long way from home."

She exhaled slowly. "A few years back, I was asked to do some work with organizations that originated during the cold war. Lots of bureaucracy falling out of an elite dictatorship that really didn't want to change. However, to capitalize on economic development opportunities, many of them had spawned smaller, fledgling companies. Now *here* is where some real change is possible." Her eyes lit up at the thought, and enthusiasm infused her voice. "Remember, it's all about money over there right now. It's the first and last thing people think about. The almighty dollar rules every facet of everyone's life. From what I saw, the singular goal is to make as much as quickly as possible."

"Sounds like home," he said.

"But this is capitalism at its rawest. Sort of a take-no-prisoners approach. Developing economies are amazing places to work."

"Aren't you some kind of governance expert? How does that kind of expertise fit in there?"

"The people running these 'new' organizations realize that to grow and prosper they have to do things differently. Employees are no longer bound for life to a designated employer out of fear of reprisal. There's lots of work, and people are figuring out that they can move and survive, even thrive. The employers are starting to realize that they are only going to make tons of money if they have the employees to do the work for them. And the employees are beginning to make it quite clear that they expect to be treated well or they are out of there."

"Good for them." He caught an eraser he had flipped high into the air.

She was starting to gain her bearings and breathe normally again. "Unfortunately, from what I saw, there are no homegrown companies to serve as inspiration or role models to the juniors with re-spect to their labor capital."

Nodding, he said, "Not surprising with past restrictions still a vivid memory."

"You got that right," she said. "Here's where I come into play. My job is to help employers get the optimum productivity out of their employees, while retaining their skilled labor for longer periods."

"Oh, is that all?" His drawling sarcasm got her attention.

She cocked her head to one side and a small grin formed at the corners of her mouth as she watched the Detective toss the eraser around. "Sounds impossible, I know," she said, "but I was impressed at how willing many of the young corporate executives were to look at new ways of doing things. There was one very interesting dilemma I encountered right away."

Raising his eyebrows, he inquired with the same friendly sarcasm, "One?"

She ignored his comment and went on. "Their understanding of democracy is different from ours, so I had to stay away from that term completely when talking about governance options. Instead, I incorporated 'collaborative governance' as the operative terminology. Lots of companies in our country have adopted that process with great results. I thought maybe I could soft sell that in a foreign land and get people working together more cooperatively."

He stopped flipping the eraser for a moment and looked directly at her. "Did it work?"

"Yes." A look of satisfaction brightened her face. "Better than I had anticipated. There's still a long way to go, but it's taking hold." She paused to think for a moment. "You know, we take for granted our involvement in the decision-making processes at so many levels in our lives in this country. Most employees of those old companies overseas wouldn't know how to participate in their futures if they were handed the reins full scale. It's not that different from the evolution of business practices in our country. Some of the old companies around here still use a pretty autocratic style."

"I see your point." He caught the eraser and squeezed it in his hand.

With less exuberance, she said, "Anyway, I was in the middle of my work, making good progress, when the call came through. 'Back to home base immediately.' No explanation." Her eyes narrowed as her face clouded in anger. "I think the Agency could use some of its own advice. They are always espousing how important transparency is in decision making."

The Detective straightened in his chair. For the first time, his voice took on a serious tone. "I'm going to need a lot of help from you. To tell you the truth, I'm not exactly sure why I'm here. This whole governance scene is kinda new to me. All I know is that I'm at your disposal."

The Researcher tilted her head and looked at her new colleague. "From the briefing we just had, something tells me your skill set is ideally suited for the task ahead. I'm still amazed at what you were able to learn about our assignment in a few short hours before our briefing, and with no information whatsoever."

The Detective smiled at the compliment and returned to his slouched position.

Folding her arms across her chest, she said, "Okay, Mister, your turn. What's your story?"

"It's pretty simple," he said. "I was working, might I say happily, in the Corporate Fraud Unit, ferreting out the bad guys and bringing them to justice, as one might say. Lots to do. More than I had anticipated when I started. Never-ending array of nefarious crimes to sort through." He grinned at his choice of terminology. "The team I worked with was great, cracking all kinds of cases. Sure hated to leave them in the lurch . . ." A grim look passed over his face. He leaned back in his chair and continued. "You hear about the kind of work we do all the time. More and more of these cases are being prosecuted. Us undercover guys are in the background and, thankfully, never mentioned in the public realm. It allows us to move from case to case." He stopped to think for a second and then looked straight into her green eyes. "I was ripped away from a pretty high-powered case to help you out. That's what got me thinking that the Agency got in over its head on this one."

She nodded and sat back in her chair. "Yeah, the Agency can be quite arrogant at times, and that can lead to complacency on their part. I have a sneaking suspicion both of these factors are at play here."

While methodically twirling a pen around and around between his fingers, he nonchalantly said, "I gathered from the briefing that they would like this one to be kept nice and quiet – probably would like it to go away, if at all possible."

"Hmm," she said, staring into space. "The only problem is that this one must be starting to make waves, or we wouldn't be here. Whatever it is, it has probably gone on way too long."

"Agreed."

"I wonder if they're actually willing to take the necessary action should we discover something untoward during our investigation?" She looked at the Detective for a second before sighing and answering her own question. "I have to be honest with you; I don't think they have the inclination or the guts to do that. They rarely do."

He stopped twirling his pen and furrowed his brow. "Then what are we here for? Seems like an expensive proposition to just cover it up."

Slowly nodding her head in agreement, the Researcher mused, "Now that's the million-dollar question, isn't it?"

The Agency

"Do you think they can do this?"

"They are the best."

"The briefing was pretty obscure."

"Meant to be."

"A rather odd combination, wouldn't you say?"

"Not for the mess we are in."

"Is the anonymous source contained?"

"Seems to be for now."

"Have the media caught a whiff of this yet?"

"No, but they will."

"We must get the facts before some reporter does."

"That is the plan."

"Is a strategy under development to get rid of this problem?"

"Yes."

"*And,* I trust our plan will include how not to let this happen again."

The Organization

"Okay, let's get going on this thing," she said, throwing her suit jacket over her oversized chair. "The quicker we wrap up this assignment, the quicker we get back to our lives."

"You got it, Search."

"Search?" She wrinkled her nose in disapproval.

"Fits the scenario, don't you think?"

She couldn't help but chuckle. *It sure beats the overused doctor title,* she thought. She began quietly drumming her fingers on her desk. "That was one brief briefing," she said.

"And vague."

"That's for sure. It makes me a little suspicious. The Agency is up to something."

"Kind of like a game of hide-and-seek. Makes me feel right at home," the Detective said as he put his legs up on his desk and folded his hands behind his head.

"From what I gathered, our assignment is to find out why one particular board deteriorated over a six-year period, bringing the Organization they represent into disrepute – and, I might add, having an effect on the Agency's reputation too. Something must have happened to magnify this situation for the Agency. My guess is that someone high up must be putting some real heat on them to put this much effort, not to mention money, into something that is usually just swept away. What does it look like to you?"

"Sums it up pretty well, I'd say. Now fill me in on what you know up to this point."

She leaned her elbows on her desk and propped her chin in her hands.

"About six years ago, I was doing some work for the Agency on board governance, determining the elements of a strong board and the structures and processes within the board that would support the development of a strong governing entity. At the time the Agency said it wanted to use this information as a template in its board member selection and training programs."

He could tell by the look on her face that she felt duped. "You doubt that now, don't you?"

"You never know what the Agency is up to. The Organization, which is the focus of our assignment, was at that time considered the model for all others to emulate. There was a strong board chair, strong president, committed and dedicated board members, and a strong senior administration. They were actively and officially incorporating the elements of collaborative governance into all aspects of their operation." Leaning back in her chair, she folded her arms across her chest. "Actually, I was quite impressed. Not only were they great on paper, they were great in person. I'm still trying to get my head around what could possibly have happened."

"What's the plan?"

She noticed his relaxed demeanor and smiled. "First, we need to develop a chronology of activities and see where the blanks are. There are going to be a lot of blanks. Six years is a long time. Then, we go to work on piecing this whole thing together. I'm really going to need your undercover skills to get deep into the relationships of the board members and management."

"Any thoughts on how I might represent myself?"

"Good question." She pulled on her lower lip as she thought for a moment. "How do you feel about being a foreign associate working with me on an analytical update of the major elements of governance systems utilized by organizations in our country?"

"Sounds good . . . I think." He scratched his head. "Have to admit, didn't quite understand what you said. This academic stuff is all above my lowly head. But, hey, give me an excuse to be quiet, naive, and nonthreatening, and I'm your guy."

"You'd also have to be charming and low key." A slight smile played on the corners of her mouth.

"Hey, Search, when you get to know me better, you'll see how natural those qualities really are," he said with feigned arrogance.

They both had a good laugh that relieved some of the tension that had developed earlier after the hasty way they had been thrown together for their "surprise" mission.

Governance Defined

"Before we go any further, Search, you have to explain this governance concept to me so I know exactly what we're up against."

"Of course." She frowned at her oversight. "I'm sorry about that. I just started getting so focused on the mission that I forgot this is all new to you."

Collecting her thoughts, she began explaining as succinctly as she could. "In a nutshell, governance is all about the structures and processes that an organization puts in place to assist with making decisions about the direction and welfare of the organization. The ultimate purpose is to enhance success and manage risk. Without such mechanisms in place, an organization would be in chaos. How the process functions is the major factor determining success. Does that make sense?"

He held his hands up. "Clear so far."

"Most importantly, the quality of that governance is directly related to the people who participate. It's kind of like a polyarchal democracy. Representatives of the target group are given the power to decide issues and determine policies and such on behalf of the entire group. These decisions, we call them allocations, are supposed to be made with the good of the whole in mind so that everyone will find them acceptable or authoritative. At least that's the hope."

"Sounds awful grandiose to me."

She wrinkled her nose in acknowledgement. "Yeah, it does, doesn't it? Well, recruitment to these positions is to motivate into active participation those individuals who meet the favored criteria. Roles in political structures are usually obtained as a result of interaction between individual ambitions and the structural opportunities available. It's a testy balance."

"So, in this case, the criteria are determined by the Agency, which has the oversight for the recruitment process and is ultimately accountable for the performance of its recruits and the outcomes they create."

"You got it. That's really good. Loyalty and political reliability are common factors."

"Just like in the corporate fraud business."

She winced at the comparison to criminal activity. "Board members can have a substantial effect on the culture of an organization. I'll bet the recruitment went awry somewhere along the line in this case, eventually creating a backlash in the Organization."

"Is that the hypothesis we're testing, Search?"

"Hmm, we'll have to see. I have found that to be a common element when boards get into trouble."

"Another similarity to my line of work. The bad guys get sloppy or too cocky, and bam!" – he slapped his hand against the desk for effect – "they get slammed in the face by the very people they put in place to protect them."

"The politics can drive you mad," she said. "The board has the legal authority to allocate funds, values, policies, and so on for the organization they represent. This allocative authority that is invested in boards provides all kinds of opportunity for abuse. It's actually amazing it doesn't happen more often."

"We really do have a lot in common, Search. The abuse of authority is how my clientele get themselves into trouble all the time."

Chuckling, she asked, "Does this give you a better idea of what we're up against?"

"From what I've gathered, fraud would be defined in this case, more or less, as deception and/or misrepresentation of the role required by the board to direct and control the organization under their authority. The major concern revolves around governance issues and whether the board was fulfilling its role."

"That pretty much sums it up," she said. "I like the analogy. I've never quite thought about it like that, but it works."

"At least it explains my brand-new title." He pointed to his security badge and gave her a mischievous grin.

"I've been wondering about that. Forensic Governance Operative?"

"Yeah, can you believe it? Bloody bureaucracy wanted to make sure I was properly identified."

"Spiffy. I think I'll call you just plain *Gov.*"

He groaned in reply.

"It's only fair, you know."

WHAT ARE YOU THINKING?

◆ ◆ ◆

What is your understanding of board governance?

What have you done to prepare yourself for your role as a board member?

Do you understand the ramifications of your decision to become a board member? Explain.

The Investigation Begins

Following a quick break to organize their office more efficiently and test the assortment of technology at their disposal, the Researcher and the Detective started sorting through the boxes of files that had been neatly stacked in one corner of the office near the door.

"I remember that board chair from six years ago when I first worked with this board," the Researcher said while looking over an old, organizational chart. "Mr. Wilson, what a gentleman. He carried himself in a casual yet distinguished manner. He had a thick head of white hair and unusually straight shoulders. He made people feel comfortable right from the start. There were no airs about this man."

She paused to remember. "Nearing retirement from his business, Wilson was well placed in the community and seen as a leader in the corporate world too. He had such sound understanding of the basic role of the board and his responsibilities as chair. He was committed to the Organization, and easy to work with – open, thoughtful, and respectful."

"Wonder what happened to change that?" the Detective said while flipping through a pile of files on his lap as he leaned back in his old, wooden chair with his feet on his desk.

The Researcher paused for a moment. Leaning on her desk, squinting in concentration, she tried to devise a theory that might shed some light. "I'm not sure, but I can tell you that board and that company were firing on all cylinders six years ago. All of the other organizations I analyzed for that project were in awe over this one. They were even asked to speak all over the globe about their governance principles. It's hard to believe that things deteriorated to the extent that they are actually under investigation."

Without looking up, he replied, "All I know is that something big must be up, or we wouldn't be here, especially me, undercover. By the way, these org charts are really extensive. Gives us lots of information." Flipping through the pages, he could see why she had been impressed.

Exasperated, she blurted out, "Gov, I tell you, they had it all covered: board committees for finance and audit, compensation, governance, board development, R&D, market development. Each committee was led by an experienced member, and senior management was included wherever appropriate. Staff was treated professionally and respectfully – their opinions really mattered. From what I observed, working relationships among these groups were excellent. These were happy people!"

"What we have here is definitely a fall from grace," he said, still flipping through the documents.

"More like a crash."

"What was the president of the day like?"

"Charismatic, strong willed, and considered arrogant by many. Smythe had a medium build and blonde hair that had broad streaks of grey in it. He always had a bounce in his step. I have no doubt that both the board and his staff relied on his strong leadership capabilities. He did a good job, and Wilson found a way to get along well with him. No sparks there. The president loved the limelight, while the chair was content to be more low key. It worked well for them."

Flipping through more notes, the Detective added, "According to these documents, Wilson finished his term a year after you did your research. From then until now, there have been two more chairs and one more president." He raised his eyebrows. "And lots and lots of turnover at the senior management level."

"The latter is what really concerns me." Her face clouded over. "A sure sign of trouble."

The Detective kicked his feet off the desk and stood up. "Enough paperwork. I'm ready to get on the road. How about we meet the current board chair and president to get the formalities out of the way. Then we can really get to work."

WHAT ARE YOU THINKING?

◆◆◆

Would ongoing turnover at the
management level concern you? Why?
Why not?

When would this become a red flag?

What would you do about it?

Back in their office the following day, the Researcher and the Detective started comparing notes from their joint meeting with the current president, Prim, and the board chair, Sackmaster.

"Well, Gov, what did you think?" She wondered if he had picked up on the same messages during their meeting.

"That was tense. Polite but awkward. Did you notice their body language?" He shook his head in disgust. "Prim was practically squirming in his seat. And that look on his face! Like he wanted to be anywhere but there. On the other hand, Sackmaster was dominant, almost desperately so."

"It was as if she had to show her prowess through her positional power. She didn't come away sounding very smart. Did you notice any sexual tension?"

"Not at all. Those two definitely only tolerate each other – on a good day."

"I agree, Gov. That's one less element we have to deal with."

"Wonder how their relationship permeates through the rest of the Organization?"

"It has to have some effect, especially on the senior staff. Now I'm really curious." Studying her partner for a second, she added, "Okay, time to do your magic, Gov. Ready to go undercover and find out what's up?"

"You bet. Did you notice they politely ignored me for most of the meeting? Their focus was on you and your work. You intimidated them, Search." He winked at her to lighten things up.

"Yeah, right." She got up from her desk and turned off her computer. "While you are doing your thing, I am going to connect with the second board chair." She sifted through some papers. "Here it is," she said. "Her name is Fall." She selected a couple of pages and tucked them into her purse. "Then I'll track down some of the retired board members. These folks are usually happy to share their experiences and perspectives. It seems to make them feel important and valued, and some keep fairly close ties with the Organization and those that succeed them. They could be a good source of info."

"It's a plan. See you in a couple days."

Preliminary Analysis

Two days later, the Researcher and the Detective met at the main door of their office building and walked through the long, seemingly deserted maze of hallways that led to their office. They chatted amicably about the beautiful autumn weather and shared a laugh about their "secret" operation. When they reached their office, they got right to work.

"I got some background information regarding Fall that may give us a start." The Researcher pulled her notes up on a handheld device as she settled her small frame into her large chair.

"Me too." The Detective grinned knowingly. "You go first."

"This is interesting stuff. Much more fun than I had anticipated."

He raised his eyebrows, questioning her change of heart.

Gesturing with her hands in surrender, she said, "Since we're stuck here, I thought we might as well enjoy ourselves."

He liked the way her eyes glinted and that her voice took on a feigned ominous tone.

"After the departure of Wilson, things changed dramatically. He had fulfilled his term, and Fall had taken over amid some controversy. Apparently Fall had campaigned relentlessly for the chair position and was granted it over a mature, long-standing business guy." Before her partner could ask the obvious, she quickly added, "The president and board were concerned that she would be a big problem if she was not given the chair position, and they didn't want to deal with the impending fallout."

"Good reason to put someone in a leadership role, don't you think?"

Ignoring his sarcasm, she continued. "Fall was very dominant. She clearly reveled in her perceived power and used the word *change* ad nauseam." The Researcher clutched her throat and stuck out her tongue. "Fall firmly believed that change was the answer to everything, and anyone who did not believe in change was wrong or bad."

"What kind of change?"

"That's the strange part. It was never defined according to the retired board members I spoke with. They didn't have a clue. She wasn't very visionary from what I gathered. Just very, very verbose. I guess she liked the sound of the word. She probably picked up the change terminology at some workshop, and it made her feel important and knowledgeable. I've seen that happen a million times with people new to a field."

The Detective moved his tall frame around in his chair, trying to find a comfortable position. "A little knowledge, and suddenly they're experts."

"You got it. For the good news, apparently Fall did conduct a professional meeting. But the board was remiss to question anything she said or to suggest alternatives. They quickly learned that any dissention perceived or otherwise, resulted in a lecture or embarrassing rebuttal."

"So they just gave up?" he asked.

"Uh huh. Too much trouble. They all led busy lives, and this was not a priority for them."

"They actually said that?"

"Yes. It seemed like no big deal," she said.

"Glad to hear our boards are handled so professionally. Gives me a great deal of comfort." He folded his arms and leaned back in his chair, shaking his head.

Smiling at his sarcasm, she felt a need to defend boards in general. "Remember, this is but one board. There are so many really dedicated folks out there protecting and furthering their organizations."

"Yeah, yeah. From where I sit, Search, there's not all that much difference between your clientele and mine."

She grimaced at the thought of board members being compared to fraudsters. "There's more. Management became very restricted during Fall's reign. They were sidelined in most cases and far less involved than with Wilson. They were either removed from board committees or their committees that reported to the board were shut down, wholesale. One board member described management as looking extremely uneasy during their encounters with Fall. They never knew what she would come up with next or how they would be belittled or publically humiliated as a result."

Unfolding his arms, the Detective sat up in his chair and scowled. "That sounds unusual for senior staff. My work takes me into all sorts of executive offices, and those guys are rarely what I would call meek. Quite the opposite."

Without looking up from her computer, she replied, "When your confidence is dashed over and over again, it takes its toll." Moving to a new document, the Researcher continued. "I also did some document analysis to see if much has changed on paper since my first visit. It looks pretty much the same – a few small changes, nothing consequential. Board development is supposedly still front and center. Fall had instituted retreat opportunities for management and the board to get to know one another better. It looks progressive *on paper*."

"So, what's bugging you?" he asked, leaning forward on his desk.

She liked how perceptive he was and how he went straight to the point. "Something just doesn't add up. Fall was dominant, very dominant, and seemed to be wielding the perceived power of the position as a personal ego boost. Her confidence was extreme. She was described as smiling and friendly on the surface but a barracuda underneath." She stopped and stared into space.

"And?"

Shaking her head to get her thoughts back to the present, she said, "That stuff really doesn't bother me. I've seen all sorts of styles and personalities that can work. It's just that she had an almost sinister desire to be viewed as important." She looked at her partner, and her voice took on a sad tone. "My goodness, she must be one unfilled person."

"Here's the scoop from my end, Search. Maybe this will help." Scrolling down his handheld device, he said, "Did you know that the current president was selected by Fall?"

She shrugged. "That would make sense. The board is responsible for the selection of the president."

"No, I mean Prim selected him personally, with the emphasis on *personally*."

"Oh!"

"From what I was told, Fall was almost exclusively responsible for the selection of Prim."

"That should have been virtually impossible," she said. "Their governance principles are specific and detailed. I know. I helped them revise their policies and procedures back six years ago when I first met this board."

"For an Organization that purports to be so open, the selection was held very close to the chest by Fall. Most of the board didn't know what was going on until the end. By that time, Fall had already made up her mind. This will come as no surprise to you, but with her dominant personality, the rest of the board gave in."

She groaned. "And so the sordid tale began."

"The only ones who raised concerns were staff members. From what I heard, they were soundly dismissed, even senior management. Boy, she could be a tyrant behind her guise of friendly servitude. Her relationship with the president is close to this day."

Seeing the twinkle in his eye, the Researcher asked, "A little too close perhaps?"

"Oh yeah. Not one person I spoke with turned down the opportunity to get in their jibes. Not much of a secret."

"Do you think her attraction to him was a factor in the selection process?"

"Yep, without a doubt. As you saw, he's quite a good-looking guy, a self-described ladies' man, I'm told. She, on the other hand, is plain and plump. He was in trouble in his past company, apparently on his way out. Situation sounded kinda desperate. His attention to her is thought to have figured prominently in his selection. Could be why she is so protective of him." Grinning like a Cheshire cat, he happily concluded, "Looks like we've landed in the middle of a daytime soap, Search. You're right; this could be fun."

The Researcher was processing the information he had provided, and she didn't like where her thoughts were going. "Just a minute here, Gov. Do you mean to say we have a jealousy ring going on here?"

She looked so distressed that he laughed out loud.

"Please tell me I'm wrong," she said. "As a woman, this is not what I want to hear."

"Sorry, Search. Seems to be the case. Sackmaster –"

"*Mrs.* Sackmaster," she corrected.

"Oh, yes, I forgot."

They both rolled their eyes and laughed, remembering how overzealous Chair Sackmaster had been when emphasizing her marital status, and the importance she believed she deserved from that relationship. Others who had been interviewed intimated that she had been selected for her role based solely on the status of her husband in the community and that she had done nothing of importance in her own life to qualify for the chair position.

"Anyway, Sackmaster is spitting mad that she is stuck with Fall's president and that she can't get rid of Fall to make Prim her own new best friend. Much to the chagrin of Sackmaster, the president continues to use Fall as his confidante regularly." He chuckled. "Apparently, Fall and Sackmaster do not get along. They are all lovey-dovey in public but are very critical of one another behind the scenes." Raising his eyebrows for emphasis and laughing, he added, "I mean *very* critical."

"It's not funny," the Researcher said, feeling deflated. "It sounds kind of yucky and sad, all at the same time."

"Can't help myself. This is bizarre. You gotta see the humor in it. And, unlike in my regular line of work, nobody is getting killed or jailed."

She saw his point and lightened up. "It sure puts a new twist on any research I've conducted," she said. "No wonder the Agency is doing this so hush-hush. What a heyday the press would have with this! It has all the elements of a good novel."

Still grinning, he asked, "What else did you find out?"

"Actually, you've already answered some of my questions. My meeting with Fall was productive, yet . . . unusual." Noticing the look on his face, she continued, "Yes, yes, she is rather plain." Murmuring under her breath, she added, "As if that should matter."

He grinned in acknowledgement. "I know. But believe me, it does."

"Where was I?" she said. "Oh, yes, Ms Fall. She was actually a gracious host, enthusiastic and effusive about her time on the board. But as I mentioned earlier, she had an edge to her. I can't quite put my finger on it. There was always a lingering doubt in my mind about the accuracy of the information she was providing."

"You mean she lied?"

"I love the way you hit issues head-on," she replied dryly. "Not necessarily. More like she saw the situation differently than the actual circumstances. Or she purposely put her own spin on the situation, believing that her audience, in this case me, was not as smart as she and thus would believe whatever she said." Batting her eyelashes, she added, "You know I'm just an innocent little scientist."

"Now who's being sarcastic?" he said, throwing his head back with laughter.

"It's my turn," she retorted, then continued more seriously. "I get the impression that the leadership style she employed during her tenure was inconsistent and self-serving. No wonder management was off balance. They never knew how she would interpret a situation."

"Have to admit, Search, your instincts are corroborating the information I was given."

"There is no doubt she loved the perceived power of the position. My first alert was her overuse of the word *I* with respect to the Organization's accomplishments. That's not usually how former board chairs speak. They seldom profess that *they* deserve the credit for the work of the administration and other staff. She even had the audacity to say that she felt she would have made the best president for the company."

"I didn't know she was from the field," the Detective said.

"She's not – not even close. She's the VP of a really small, nondescript institution. All of her other experience has been in entry or barely midlevel jobs. She's a facade."

"Sounds rather full of herself," he said.

"She has a very forceful personality, so I can see how she manipulated people. She's a master at putting on the right face for the right people. I've seen so much of that recently in my work, both here and overseas."

"Essential ingredient, I'd say, no matter where you are on the planet." He flicked a ball of paper into the trash can.

"Her relationship with the president is a bit . . . off balance. She absolutely effused about him and extolled his virtues many a time during our conversation, even when the discussion had nothing to do with him. She was overly protective and defensive in every way. On the other hand, she was not very complimentary about Smythe, his predecessor."

Leaning his head on his hand, the Detective said, "I take it they didn't get along?"

She shook her head and replied, "Two dominant personalities both wanting the spotlight. From what I heard, they had many battles. Smythe thought he would be able to control her because of her inexperience. She thought she knew it all and was just as stubborn as he."

"That never lasts. One of them had to leave. We both know who that was." More paper wads were launched at the trash.

"At least it wasn't a bloodbath," she said. "Fortunately, Smythe saw the light and moved on to bigger and better things. He would have had a tough time trying to depose her. Rarely has that ever happened." She shifted in her chair and stretched to loosen some tense muscles.

"Did she say anything else that might help?"

"You know, Gov," she said, squinting, "it wasn't so much what she said, exactly, but what she emphasized and how she said things. She described in detail how the board operated, what a wonderful job they did. If you didn't know better, you would have thought she ran the place."

He grinned at the seeping cynicism. He liked her subjective interjections, especially since she clearly felt guilty about them.

"The thing that really made me take notice was her criticism of senior management in almost every way," she continued. "Those poor folks, as experienced and successful as they were, couldn't do anything right in her mind. It was as if their accomplishments somehow demeaned the current president's status. Apparently a great deal of high-profile success had been achieved prior to President Prim's arrival, and he was none too pleased about the attention that garnered from the press and other like organizations. It seemed as if she was determined to make sure that past successes were diminished so that nothing got in the way of the status of her president."

"Yet another factor in support of our jealousy theory." He tossed a larger wad of paper over his shoulder into a more distant receptacle. He looked to see if he made his shot, then added, "I think we might have the *key message* you've been searching for."

Flopping back in her chair, she said, "Well, here's another one for you. Fall wasn't willing to talk about Wilson, the former chair, at all. She dismissed him entirely, even when I asked her directly about her experience on the board while he was there."

"You liked that guy, right?"

"Oh yes. I respected him as well. In all my work, he has to count as one of the strongest chairs I have seen, in almost every way."

"Fall really has a self-esteem problem."

Nodding her head, she said, "No doubt. At first blush, I would say the problems for this organization started relatively soon after Fall took over. I've got to talk with some of the other board members to confirm my initial observations."

"I think I can help there, Search. After our meeting with Sackmaster and Prim, I casually walked around the main headquarters of the company to talk to staff. You would have been proud," he said, grinning. "Low-key and humble only begin to describe my manner."

She rolled her eyes.

"Yes, I must say," he continued while dusting off the lapel of his jacket, "charmed the pants off them."

"But did you actually uncover any useful information?" she asked, enjoying his humor.

"Yep. Most of the staff had no idea who the board chair was and didn't really care. There was no perceived impact on their work. Regarding the president, they saw him as harmless, and the word *shallow* was used several times. Apparently it was quite common for Prim to try to use his good looks to gain favor."

"Where have I heard that before?" she asked dryly.

"But that's small stuff. I've got pay dirt for you, Search." He sat upright in his chair, eager to tell more. "Ran into a VP who invited me to a service club meeting with him. Sounds pretty benign, eh?" His eyes twinkled in delight, and his voice took on a lilting tone. "This is where things get interesting. You wouldn't believe how many current and former board members I met at just one meeting. That private club seems to be the recruiting ground for this board. Has to be."

"A den of iniquity?" She was enjoying the melodrama.

"You might say that. This VP, Dung, was polite but guarded, almost fearful around the directors. There's no doubt he knows what's going on, but apparently he has problems of his own. Can't quite do the job – too soft. Wants others to do his tough work for him, which has lost him a lot of support. Unfortunately, he blames his colleagues for his imminent demise and is trying his darndest to undermine them to save himself."

"My goodness!" the Researcher said with disgust. "Is no one capable of running that Organization? I might as well be back in a developing economy. At least there I can anticipate the moves."

The Detective chuckled. "This is where the other two VPs and the rest of senior management come into play. They kept the place running while the crazies did their nastiness." The playfulness left his voice and his face clouded.

"What's wrong, Gov?" she asked, unable to hide the concern in her voice. This wasn't like him at all.

"President Prim and the board fired one of the VPs a while back." He looked up at her. "Vinn, the young one with all the promise and the accomplishments to boot."

"Oh no, don't tell me! Another victim of the jealousy factor?"

"Sure looks like it," he said. "The third remaining VP, Bentley, had chosen to take early retirement before that hit the fan. Apparently he was disgusted by what was transpiring around him and quietly left. He sure was respected."

"Smart move."

"No doubt about it."

They were both silent for a moment. Then the Detective sat up straight, ready to continue his story. He cleared his throat for effect, and the lilt returned to his voice. "Using my new position as your foreign associate, the board members at this meeting were more than happy to talk about their experiences. Actually, they seemed delighted. Discovered a few things that might help us out."

Looking over at her partner with admiration, she said, "You did have a productive couple of days. You're really picking up on the underpinnings of this case. I wish I could say the same," she said, sighing heavily.

"Hey, Search, you've done great. Remember, you're out in the open, leading our charade. You're the expert they're fawning all over. You have to be careful. On the other hand, I have full range of motion. No one knows or cares about me and my opinions. They care about what you're up to. Have no doubt, they're watching you. As far as they know, I'll be returning to my own country soon, never to be seen again. I'm safe for them."

"Thanks, Gov. But there are still so many questions to be answered."

"I think it's time for lunch. You hungry?" he asked.

"Starving."

WHAT ARE YOU THINKING?

◆◆◆

How much power should board
chairs have?

Would you question the qualifications
or behaviors of a board chair? If so,
under what circumstances?

What person or persons would you
approach with your concerns?

Digging Deeper

It was mid-afternoon, and most of the lunch crowd had dispersed. They took their time walking down the treed street. There was little conversation. The fresh air did them both good: his fidgeting diminished, and her head cleared. Eventually they found a small bistro that had few customers.

"Mmmm, good food," she said. Eating always had a calming effect on her.

Digging into his sandwich with gusto, he asked, "By the way, Search, did you get a chance to meet with Prim and Fall again yesterday?"

"Yes, I met with them individually. They were very different with me this time round. Prim did the charmer thing you mentioned and even tossed his blond mane a time or two." She shook her head. "Who does he think I am? Some bimbo who happens to do research for a living?"

"They said he was shallow."

"It's obvious that he has had considerable success with that approach in the past," she said, referring to her notes between bites. "He lamented about his experiences with Fall, who hired him. He was sad when she had to leave after three years. Apparently she took a new position that had some potential for conflict with her board work. Interestingly, just like the board members, he spoke frequently about her focus on change in the Organization."

Repressing a small chuckle, she added, "Even he seemed irritated with this constant talk of change for the sake of change. I can tell you this: he was none too pleased with her expectation of him to change something big somewhere, including a noticeable change at the executive level, just to show the world that change was happening. Believe me, Prim knew full well that a couple of the vice presidents, namely Bentley and Vinn, were holding him up and doing his tough work for him."

"Change for the sake of change, huh? Prim and Fall are both selfish, aren't they?"

"Sad, but true. Fall desperately wanted to make her mark. It shows her lack of experience."

"Poisoned by her first taste of power," he said. "Now, *that* I've seen a hundred times in the fraud business. Like an addiction of sorts. Usually comes from a sense of insecurity or lack of basic confidence." Angling his chair toward her, he stated gravely, "Never ends good."

The Researcher nodded. "Gov, I can tell you this with certainty: there is no love lost between Prim and his predecessor, Smythe. He had this disgusted look on his face every time I asked about the past. Yet those were the glory years of the business." She paused, frowning. "When I think about it, he often had a disgusted look on his face. He couldn't give anyone credit for anything. How does someone like that make it to the top? He would drive the ambition right out of me. I'd want to wipe that disgusted look right off his face."

He couldn't help but smile to himself at the thought of her completing that task. "Sounds like more jealousy to me, Search. You see it more often than people are willing to admit."

"It's natural that someone coming into a well-functioning company would like to put their own stamp on it, but this was rather ugly."

"Did he say much about Chair Sackmaster?" he asked.

"Only to say that they had sent her on a number of international trips the past couple of years. Apparently the limelight is very important to *Mrs.* Sackmaster as well."

"From what I heard, those trips keep her from interfering too much in the company. Makes her feel important," he said. "That organization is loaded with prima donnas!"

"No doubt." Wiping her fingers on a napkin, she scrolled down her notes. "Oh yeah, this is interesting. When I spoke about governance and leadership generically, Prim was much more forthcoming. He expressed his concerns about the lack of experience and background of some board members that could lead to challenges within the Organization. He was eager to give his opinion of how organizations should be run, and the things that other organizations did wrong. It was really phony. He was trying so hard to impress me, he sounded silly."

Suppressing a grin, the Detective said, "Probably wanted a lot more than that from you." Before she could comment, he changed the subject. "What about Sackmaster? Did you get anything out of her?"

She shook her head in amusement. "You might say I did. She was uncomfortable around me, that's for sure. She is a tall, attractive woman and on the surface looks the part of the leader. But she has no depth."

He finished the last bite of his lunch, feeling much better. "Think I can help there. From what I was told, she has no postsecondary education whatsoever, and no business development experience to counter that, or even any substantial charity work. Her only claim to fame is her association with her spouse."

"Gov, I have to tell you that that's no excuse for her poor behavior as board chair. She accepted the position knowing full well what she was getting into."

"Correction. Apparently she actively sought the position just like Fall did. Promised all sorts of things to some of the weaker board members. From what I was told, she was desperate for the position. Even petitioned the president."

Annoyed with yet another self-serving board chair, the Researcher said, "That gives her even less of a reason for her poor performance. I have seen lots of board chairs and board members in general who do not have the qualifications you mentioned, often in smaller communities that do not have the recruitment bases of larger places. Yet they are serious about their work, care deeply about their organizations, and most importantly, know when to get help. They often surround themselves with folks who have the desired expertise. They use the talents of the senior staff. I have seen much success in many instances. Mutual respect is achieved in no time."

"Nonetheless, it's clear she lacks confidence," he said, "and that would explain the arrogance she emitted when we first met. Tried to compensate by showing she was in charge when the president was there. Bottom line – her selection for the chair position is a bit suspect, to say the least. That makes two in a row," he said, holding up two fingers.

"Both are intimidated by well-educated and accomplished individuals. They use their perceived power to try to compensate for their lack of skills and expertise, and they try desperately to control what they don't understand."

"Sad, but true."

"That would explain Sackmaster's nervousness at our last meeting," she said. "She was out of her element entirely. She flippantly talked about some contracting work she had done before she joined the board, in an attempt to show she was qualified to be the chair, but it was pretty vague. I felt really sorry for her. It was pathetic. She talked incessantly about the work she had done for the organization and her international trips. No specifics. I hate to say this, but she didn't come across as being very smart. The thing she was most proud of was the length of the board meetings. She said she ran the shortest meetings ever and beamed at this *achievement.*"

"That might not be so bad. Who wants to sit through long, boring meetings?"

"I don't think most folks do. However, my concerns focus around due diligence. If her primary objective was to race through meetings, was the board fulfilling the responsibilities they had accepted?"

"Okay," he said, raising his hands in surrender. "I see your point, Search. There has to be a balance there."

She ignored him and went on. "I understand that people are tired from their *real* jobs and just want to get home. But if boards race through issues without background information, without the opinions and thoughts of management or other board members, without really understanding the issues at hand, they are being negligent and need to be held accountable. No one is forcing them to be on the board. They made the choice. That darn Agency, where have they been all this time?"

"Talk about accountability . . ." The Detective let his voice trail off.

Glad to have that off her chest, she said, "So, where to next for you, Gov?"

Casually sitting back in his chair with his hands behind his head, he answered nonchalantly, "Got an invitation to their fundraiser tomorrow evening."

Her eyes lit up. "That's good! That will give you more time to ferret out these relationships we've discovered."

"You?"

"I'm going to meet with as many board members as I can to see what's up from a *professional perspective*, shall we say. Something President Prim said when we met rings a warning bell in my mind. He spoke of his involvement in board member selection and in the selection of Sackmaster as chair. I want to see how the other board members see the recruitment process. This could be the crux of the whole thing." She grimaced. "I sure hope I don't have to meet with Sackmaster again. She's dangerous. When someone feels out of their element, they look for ways to look important or to assert their authority. Thankfully, I don't work in the administration."

"I'm with you, Search."

"And you know, Gov, it might be a good idea for me to call that retired vice president, Bentley. I'll bet he knows more than we think. He was around a long time."

"Member of the private club?" He was getting more and more concerned about that connection.

"I don't know yet."

WHAT ARE YOU THINKING?

◆ ◆ ◆

What do you think went wrong in the
chair selection process?

How should the process be conducted?

Should the president be involved in
board member or chair selection?
Why? Why not?

The Agency

"Progress is being made?"

"Yes, the calls have started."

"Making some waves are they?"

"More than anticipated."

"Safe to continue?"

"For now."

"Monitor this closely. No mistakes."

"Understood."

Patterns Emerge

Two days later, the Detective strolled into the office and made himself comfortable at his desk. The Researcher was absorbed in her work and barely looked up when she said, "So, Gov, how did the fundraiser go?"

"Lovely evening, I must say. They were nice to me for the most part, but those board members, former and current, sure do have high opinions of themselves. They described their service club as being made up of the do-gooders and the *real* business people –"

"*Of course* they were in the latter group?" she interjected.

"Of course, though some of them have very little experience in the business world. There was this one guy who is in his last term as a director. Nasty guy. Spoke negatively about senior management every chance he got. No qualifications for the board, from what I gathered, other than belonging to this private club and being friends with a couple of board members on the selection committee. Seems to hate one vice president in particular, Vinn."

"Let me guess. He was intimidated by her?"

"Oh yeah. Went after her like a piranha. Apparently couldn't make any headway under Wilson, who wouldn't have anything to do with it. Saw Mr. Nasty for what he was. Unfortunately, Mr. Nasty made headway when Fall came along, but it was Sackmaster who openly backed his assessment. Actually, he doesn't like VP Dung either, but tolerates him because he's in this private club and feels he's too weak to bother them much. Guess he felt he had to keep one of them. Others might catch on if he goes after him too. He's good friends with Sackmaster."

"Weak attracts weak," she added.

"Yep, that's about it in a nutshell. Dangerous guy. What I would call a sissy bully."

She looked at him dubiously. "A sissy bully?"

"Yeah, mean and rude to the people he knows can't fight back without jeopardizing themselves. Apparently he can't hold a job due to his abrasive personality and weak skill base, and he's in the human resources business! Definitely a slimy busybody."

She chuckled at his choice of terminology. "A great role model for the employees, isn't he?" she said dryly.

WHAT ARE YOU THINKING?

◆ ◆ ◆

How have you played a role in corporate bullying? What would you do if you observed others indulging?

What would you do if a fellow board member publically berated senior management?

How would you handle a difficult board member if you were chair? If you were a director at large?

The Researcher returned to her computer in earnest, and the Detective had to prod her to answer his questions. "How did your house calls go with the board members you were planning to connect with? Make any headway?"

"More than I thought I would. Outside of a few bad seeds, most of these folks can be rather nice."

"No surprises there. I found the same thing."

She turned her computer screen in his direction. "Just a sec. Before we go on, let me show you something. This is a chart listing the board members over the past six years. This column depicts their places of employment and positions. The next shows their date of birth, terms, board committees, and so on."

He leaned forward to get a good look. "Impressive list. What I would expect for a board like this."

"Keep looking down the list."

"Ahhhh."

"What do you see?"

"A shift in the background of the board members. Lower-level positions, less prominent companies, younger."

She moved the spreadsheet over to the right a little more. "Take a look at the board committee column."

After a minute or so, he responded, "That can't be good. The same people served on the board selection committee their entire terms. And from what I gathered at the charity event, they still play a strangely influential role – like they never left."

"That supports what the board members have told me too," she said. "Those three," she indicated them with her finger, "were also the only ones allowed into the inner circle by Chair Fall during the presidential selection."

"No wonder Sackmaster is so bummed. She was excluded."

"Oh, she had her spy. That nasty HR guy you met."

Perplexed, the Detective scratched his head. "Why didn't the longer serving members of the board do something? Just look at their credentials! They have all kinds of leverage."

"I asked that question straight up. While the answers did not surprise me, the candor of the board members did," she said.

"Let me guess. The make-no-waves theory at work again?"

"Oh yeah. They know the board has deterio-rated to the point where they are only selecting very young and inexperienced members, or those with little or no real qualifications. They used the excuse that, with their educational and career backgrounds, these new members were filling in gaps on the board. I got the impression that they are waiting with bated breath for their terms to expire so they can get out of there."

WHAT ARE YOU THINKING?

◆◆◆

Would you speak up if you thought
board dynamics were deteriorating?
Why? Why not?

How would you approach the issue?

To whom would you direct your
concerns? Why?

The Detective stood up to stretch. "I take it you had some good discussions while I was sacrificing my charming self for charity."

"I sure did." Turning the computer back to face her, she partially closed the lid and took out her handheld. "Actually, Gov, I had a better time than I thought I would talking with those folks. Most of the current and past board members that I contacted were nice people and seemed to care about the Organization. The downside is, they just didn't have the time, or inclination, to focus on the politics of the Organization. No one, and I mean no one, wants to make waves. They want their CVs to be filled with the right activities, and they want to stay clean in the process."

"They really want things to be easy," he said. "If it's anything like my conversations, they sure like to talk, though. Will say almost anything to someone like me, someone safe. No guts to actually do anything, though, from what you have been saying."

The Researcher admitted that the Detective's assessment was accurate. "Unfortunately, on governing boards it's pretty typical for the members to hide their heads in the sand. A lot of the people I spoke with were aware that challenges existed, but they were happy to take the path of least resistance, even if it meant that good people were sacrificed in the process. They had no problem hiding behind the obscurity of being *on the board*. While seemingly committed during their board term, several had little desire for a long-term attachment to the company."

The Detective sat down, leaned his elbows on the desk, and thought for a moment. "You know, Search, this is how a few power-hungry, insecure folks take hold. No one cares at the time. And once they do empower themselves, they're almost impossible to depose. Works the same way in the fraud business. I found some real power pockets. Just like your list showed, I found a couple of long-time board members who have a stranglehold on the selection process. They never once mentioned the Agency, which leads me to believe they were allowed to operate on their own."

"This is looking more and more like the organizations I've studied that have autocratic cultures. Power and control from a few tiny cloisters literally dominated these organizations." Grimacing, she added, "I really thought they had evolved beyond that in this organization."

"At least here no one is getting killed for their actions. You can't say that for everywhere."

He was so matter of fact that she winced in response. "Boy, that's pretty bleak if it's the only difference we can think of," she said. Feeling deflated, she summarized what they were both thinking. "Just like the individual board members, the Agency doesn't want to make waves. The board members felt it easier to let terms expire rather than try to do anything."

A thought crossed her mind. "By the way, in contrast to what we have been told by President Prim, many were happy with the departure of Chair Fall. She drove them insane with her empty talk about change."

"Sounds like one of those people who thinks everyone should change but her." The Detective started flipping an eraser in the air.

"Oh, she definitely considered herself this great change agent. It's interesting that I couldn't discover one major change that happened during her tenure – not a policy change or a new strategic direction. Unless you count the fact that she eliminated any committee she could that contained senior management. She didn't believe the board needed to be bothered with too much association with the riffraff. It might influence board members too much."

"This has arrogance written all over it," he said. "All talk and no show?"

"Pretty much. She prides herself on her one great accomplishment: the hiring of the current president."

"Has he had any great accomplishments?" he asked as his eraser flipped out of his reach. He watched it bounce off the far side of his desk.

"Not that I could tell. His greatest feat seems to be his ability to tolerate *Mrs.* Sackmaster."

They both laughed.

After taking a couple of seconds to enjoy the moment, the Researcher turned more serious. "Actually, Gov, the retired vice president, Bentley, shed some light on this. I'm afraid he didn't have much nice to say about the guy. He said Prim created a hostile and confusing environment for the rest of the exec. He would intentionally pit the VPs against one another in terms of budget and operating issues."

"Sounds pretty normal at that level," the Detective said. "Everyone vying for what they can get."

"Apparently this was much more sinister – an intentional course of action to make sure that the VPs never formed any kind of unity."

"Sure supports how weak this guy is. Afraid his own inner circle might actually meld and do good work."

She thought his sarcasm was well placed. "I laughed when Bentley said the guy was in a constant state of disgust. I sure saw in person what that was like." She scrunched up her face. "Very distasteful. Eww. Worse, it really dashed the confidence of the VPs. He even tried to undermine their authority by assigning their middle management to new roles close to his office without the VPs even knowing until the deed had been done."

"What a creep! By the sounds of it, he used his position and concocted promises to co-opt the innocent."

She kicked the side of her desk restlessly. "And worse, they fell for it."

Calmly as ever, the Detective said, "You see it all the time in the fraud business. People just can't seem to help themselves. They see an opening to enhance their power, and in they go. Then when they get caught, it's always someone else's fault." Straightening up and stretching with a good yawn, he asked, "Find out anything more from the board members?"

Yawning in reply, she said, "For the record, Bentley, the retired VP, was never a member of that private club."

"Neither was VP Vinn," he said. "She knew what was going on there and stayed far away from it, as I was told. Didn't do her any good, though. Once she was in the sights of that evil HR guy, and with a weak president too jealous to support her, she was doomed. There were a couple of board members in particular who felt very, very guilty that they did not help her out."

"One seemingly nice guy I spoke with also noticed how many good folks they were losing in management positions and appeared quite concerned."

"So why didn't he do something about it?" It was getting harder and harder to contain the contempt he felt for these people.

Throwing her arms open in surrender, she replied, "Using your theory, no guts, I guess. The typical 'doesn't want to make waves' response."

"You'd think these comings and goings at such a high level would have been a lightning rod for the board to take notice."

"You would think so, wouldn't you? Apparently, with the board having such little direct contact with senior staff, the president had carte blanche to dismiss the leavings with one excuse or another. The godsend for this Organization was that the worker bees were oblivious to the politics and antics going on behind the boardroom door."

Rolling his shoulders to release tension, he said, "Look, Search, I gotta get out of here for a while. Too much sitting around."

Sympathizing, she asked, "Would you like to go for a walk, and we can finish this conversation?"

Without responding, he grabbed his coat off the rack and opened the door for her.

WHAT ARE YOU THINKING?

♦ ♦ ♦

What role should the board play in senior administration issues?

Would you get involved if you saw a member of senior management being treated unfairly? Why? Why not?

How is the organization as a whole affected by senior administration dynamics?

Hands in their pockets, they strolled down the parkway. The trees were starting to turn various colors, and every once in a while they could hear the rustling of busy squirrels stashing away their winter food.

"This was a good idea. The sun feels great," he said.

She smiled in agreement. "Gov, I meant to ask you earlier. Was there much talk at the fundraiser about company business from the board members in general, or was it more just negative ramblings from a couple of folks?"

"Oh, there was a lot of chatter among some of the directors. Even a couple of previous members were in on the conversation. To tell the truth, I was kinda embarrassed to be there. They were way too descriptive about some people who obviously had displeased them one way or another, and they were making decisions I had no business being party to."

Looking at her partner in disbelief, the Researcher asked, "They actually discussed personnel matters in front of you? That's kind of cocky."

"Afraid so. It was like I was invisible."

"What complete arrogance! This is worse than I thought." She nibbled on her lower lip as her mood darkened.

"It wasn't just the fact that they discussed confidential business in front of me, Search, it was the tone and content of their discussions that was disturbing. They continually made disparaging comments about certain sitting board members. And the poor administration, they got one shot after another. Even the coveted president, when Fall's cronies weren't around, got his punches. Actually, truth be told, the board thinks he's shallow, just like the staff does."

"This is getting sicker by the minute," she said. "I wish we could find some evidence to support what you've heard. I'm afraid we're not getting much help from the paperwork I've been able to find. Having reviewed the minutes from their board meetings over the past couple of years, I can tell you there isn't much to comment on. It's pretty standard stuff – presentations and motions and very, very sparse discussion notes."

"From what I saw, Search, I think most of their *work* was done behind the scenes in dark, little corners." An impish grin formed on the edges of his mouth.

"It appears rather clandestine, doesn't it?" Under her breath, she added, "It's more like what I would expect in a bad soap opera or novel."

"I've seen this a hundred times before in work with corporate fraud. There seems to be a belief among crooks that the closer they keep information and dialogue to their chests, the safer they are."

"But, in this case, what are the board members trying to achieve?" she asked. "In most cases, there are no huge payoffs in the wings."

"Small people in a small world. Somehow they got wrapped up in a power-and-control web. They purposely divided themselves into the power brokers and the lesser others. You should hear them talk when they're together."

"Just think how small and unfulfilled their lives must be." Her voice projected the disgust she felt. "The powers that be abdicated their responsibilities and let the inmates run the asylum, as they say." Looking up at the sky, she raised her voice. "Where were you, Agency?"

"Do you think it ever works in the long run?" He already knew the answer.

Sighing, she looked back at him. "That's the problem, Gov. It usually does, with respect to board governance. Based on any of the research I've ever been involved in, a case like this is an anomaly. At least it used to be." She pondered that thought for a moment.

They kept up their easy pace as a slight breeze made the leaves around them flutter. "What're you thinking?" he asked. "I see that look in your eyes."

"What look?"

"Kind of angry or frustrated or concerned or all combined. Like you know the answer but you just don't want to believe it's true. Better spit it out."

Looking down at the pathway, she waited a second and then could not help but let her feelings be known. "Oh no, Gov, do you think the Agency is taking this so seriously because it's not so much an anomaly anymore? Could this be a political epidemic?"

"Search, all I know is that when I started ferreting out corporate fraud years back, it was considered an anomaly too. Can't say that anymore, can we?" He raised his eyebrows to emphasize his point.

"The hypothesis I had formed in my mind was 'the path of least resistance.' Just like a stream flows through the least resistant substrate, the board took the direction that was the easiest."

"But not necessarily the best for the organization."

"I'm afraid not," she said. "You know, Gov, my whole career has been based on analyzing data and situations, and discovering patterns and trends. For example, the jealousy trend we spoke of earlier. The 'path of least resistance' is another."

"From what I've seen, Search, I wouldn't underestimate your intuition. You seem to see things clearly before you actually prove your position."

"Thanks, Gov. Wish I could trust myself as much as you seem to. The scientist in me wants data – and lots of it."

"Human nature and human relations are forms of data, aren't they? They seem to bubble up as hunches. In my line of work, hunches are sometimes all we have for a long time."

Kicking some leaves on the path, she said, "The more we work together, the more I understand how similar our work really is. Kind of scary actually." With a little, grudging sigh, she added, "I guess I should give the Agency a little credit for pairing us up."

He smiled. "Speaking of the Agency, still wonder about their urgency in this matter. Doesn't make much sense yet. Something snipped at them damn hard."

"Often, it's only when it bites you in the bum that you take notice. I have to admit, Gov, this is one of the most bizarre assignments I have ever been involved with."

He shrugged. "Seems about par for me."

Looking at her watch, the Researcher sucked in a deep breath. "Darn! Sorry, Gov, I have to run. I have a meeting with another board member." She turned and started to walk away quickly. "See you tomorrow?" she asked over her shoulder.

He waved, chuckling at her sudden exuberance. "Sure thing. That'll give me time to make some calls."

Glancing back, she added with a touch of playful sarcasm, "Still playing the innocent, huh?"

"Works like a charm with these people. Been going on for so long, they've become too cocky and confident to notice they've been discovered." He winked at her and she laughed, still striding away.

Synthesizing the Data

The following morning, back in the office, both quietly drank their coffee.

"What are you smiling about? Or are you grimacing?" the Detective asked.

She shook her head. "The board member I met with late yesterday was a bit fluffy."

He muted the grin starting to form on his lips. "Fluffy?"

"She was just like you see in the movies or hear about in blonde jokes. I couldn't believe it! It really sets my gender back a notch. She's completely baffled as to why she was selected for the board. Flighty and giggly, like a little girl, with big blue eyes that I'll bet have melted many a heart. She effused about how exciting it is to be on the board and about how she knows nothing."

In response to his raised eyebrows, she added, "Oh, yeah, she actually said that out loud. She couldn't figure out why she'd been selected. She was in awe of the other board members and was thrilled to be along for the ride. When she spoke of the president, she got all gushy. It was like she was in love. She never said a single word about the Organization or the work of the board. What a waste of time!"

"Indicative of our past discussions regarding the selection process," he said. "At least you confirmed what the chart showed with respect to the level of board credentials."

Slouching heavily into her chair with a big exhale, she nodded her head in agreement. "Did you have any luck with your calls?"

"Spoke at length to a friendly guy I had talked with briefly at the charity event. He hadn't stayed around for the backroom politics, so I thought it might be worth connecting with him again. Ends up he's extremely disappointed with what he sees happening around him, to the point that he has brought it up with another board member who shares his concerns."

She sat up in her chair and took off her jacket. "Thank goodness! Just when I was losing faith in the entire board."

"There's a problem, though, Search. He too belongs to that private club, and many of the people are his friends. That's why he hasn't taken any action. I don't think he's very happy."

With a look of frustration, she said, "That darn club again. I'd love to put up a sign outside their boardroom door – *DANGER: Your so-called board has become a sleazy club!"*

He smirked and nodded.

Waving off the frivolity, the Researcher opened a document on her computer. "Look here, Gov. Speaking of clubs, I added a column to our chart indicating who belongs to that private fold."

Scanning the list, he pursed his lips. "It's sure obvious when you see it like that. Youch!"

She stood up suddenly and paced the few steps she could in their shared office, letting her growing agitation show. "Okay, Gov, I've had it with the interviews and dialogue. We're just going in circles now with this soap opera. It's time to put some structure around our data. Let's summarize what we have so far."

"Works for me," he said.

"Over the course of six years, this board went from having a strong board chair, Wilson, and a strong president, Smythe, to the opposite end of the spectrum – a weak board chair, Sackmaster, and a weak president, Prim," she said, standing with her arms folded. "In my opinion, the only reason either of these people has survived is that the Organization had a strong reputation in the past, strong middle managers and staff, a favorable political environment, and a positive economic climate. Weak individuals seem to be able to hide behind these internal and external success factors as – thankfully

– they do not have the leadership skills to twist an entire Organization to their way of thinking."

He squeezed a stress ball he had found in his desk drawer to keep focused. "They just float along on the coattails of the past, which they despise, pretending to the public to be leading the way."

"You got it," she replied. "From my observations, a weak board chair will support a weak president so that they are not overshadowed and so that they feel a sense of control. The weak president looks good when there is a weak chair and vice versa, so it's the perfect symbiotic relationship."

"As long as their facade is not uncovered."

"Or," she said, leaning on her desk and looking up at him sideways, "if there is no strength of character on the board."

WHAT ARE YOU THINKING?

◆ ◆ ◆

What do you think of a private club serving as a political backroom for board members?

How should board selection be conducted to fulfill the needs of the organization?

Are you a "weak" board member? How do you know? What are you going to do about it?

The Researcher adjusted her computer so they could see the screen contents on the large blank wall of the office.

"What do you think? Are we in agreement?" the Researcher asked while her eyes never left the screen.

They studied the list silently for a few minutes, running through the information they had collected to ensure they could substantiate each item.

- Jealousy
- Corporate bullying
- Imbedded social connections
- Sexual interaction
- Power and control
- Backroom politics
- Secluded recruitment process
- 'Make no waves' culture
- Path of least resistance

Jumping up from his chair, and nearly scaring her half to death, the Detective proclaimed, "Hey, Search, let's skip all this detective work and write us a steamy novel. All we're missing is some kind of money angle. You in?"

Grinning at his antics, she replied, "Don't tempt me. That might be the only way this skuzzy mess becomes public and anyone actually does anything."

Settling back into his chair with melodramatic flare, the Detective reset his focus on the list of intervening factors. "Okay, what we do know is that these elements are all interrelated. Seems to me like the jealousy factor might have started the whole thing spinning."

Leaning back in her chair and folding her arms, she looked away from the list and at her partner seated beside her. "I agree. Let's talk about jealousy on boards for a minute. Research rarely enters into this realm because it's considered too subjective for good science."

"Let's be frank here, Search, and call a spade a spade. This may be a bigger issue than you're willing to admit."

"Oh, I admit, believe me. It's getting the participants or stakeholders to admit that's the challenge. Jealousy can be a powerful factor in board dynamics, either between board members or between senior management and board members." She thought for a moment. "I don't recall observing senior management as jealous of board members very often, but I sure have seen board members jealous of senior management. I have to admit, this is one of the most obvious cases I can recall. We have two board chairs a few years older than one of the vice presidents, same gender, few accomplishments, and an additional board member, opposite gender, also a few years older than the VP in question and no accomplishments that we know of."

The Detective interrupted. "Seems to be a couple of the essential ingredients for jealousy – being close in age and being very successful. Vinn had everything they longed for but could never have."

"Bentley, the retired VP, had a similar set of skills and personal characteristics," she said. "But he was at the tail end of his career, and she was just getting started, thus she posed more of a threat."

"Wonder what would have happened if he hadn't been able to retire?"

"Good question. He might have been their first target because he knew too much. Maybe that's what hastened his retirement. Apparently, his early departure was quite a surprise to everyone. In any case, they would have gone after him in due course, because he would be perceived as a threat to their power and control."

Shaking his head in contempt, the Detective said, "Unfortunately, the Organization had two successive board chairs – Fall and Sackmaster – with similar negative characteristics, who made it their mission to *get* at least one VP, as I overheard on numerous occasions at their lovely, private club."

"Gov, I think the 'jealousy factor' was a major determinant in this case. Dung was too weak to be much of a threat and Bentley bailed before they could touch him. With that nasty HR guy and both board chairs jealous of her accomplishments, Vinn became their target. Most bullies have a mark, a single individual they focus on. And for some reason, they just can't control themselves. They are vicious. Once that irritant is out of the way, they simply move on to their next victim. Vinn just happened to be their first."

"Corporate bullying at its worst. They purposely hired a weak president so he would be obliged to kowtow to the board chair in particular, and" – he clicked his thumb and forefinger to emphasize his point – "it was game over."

"Scumbags." The room was quiet for a long while. Then sitting up straight the Researcher again studied the list of contributing factors they had amassed. "Gov, I think I have connected all the dots. The jealousy factor was furthered by the strengthening of social interaction over several years, aided in no small part by membership in a private club. This gave ease of access and security. This is also what creates the pack mentality among teenagers that we hear so much about. Here we're calling it corporate bullying. These social interactions were imbedded in the dynamics of many of the board members."

"Take away the club factor, and you take away a good part of their means and opportunity to connive."

"And the sexual interaction strengthened key relationships and, shall we say, enhanced the social interactions of said individuals."

"Very delicately put, Search," he said while performing a mock bow.

She grinned and went on, "This sexual attraction, when enacted further, enhanced the players' sense of security and created a more confident power-and-control scenario. This enabled President Prim to do his underhanded management shuffles with no fear of reprisal from the chair, who serves as the official source of appeal for the vice presidents."

Seamlessly, he picked up where she left off in the storyline: "Enter Chair Sackmaster. She recognizes what is going on between Prim and Fall, and we have the jealousy factor raising its ugly head again. She is further incensed by young Vice President Vinn, who she sees as a possible rival who may upstage her at some point."

"The personalities of Fall and Sackmaster seem to be suited ideally to bullying," she added. As an aside she couldn't help but say despondently, "Why did they have to be women?"

Ignoring her last comment, this time it was he who stayed on track. "And, may I add, they utilized their considerable talents in this regard in a corporate forum."

"Disgusting. Just like in the schoolyard," she said. "It's odd, but you rarely hear that much about corporate bullying. It's always masked under different terminology."

"Alas, Search, it is alive and well in its rawest form."

"All right, so this pack mentality morphed into many power and control scenarios, setting the stage for the backroom politics we observed."

"Yep. And the backroom politics produced a bastardized recruitment process, which further strengthened the power and control of a few select individuals acting out their pack culture."

"Add the make-no-waves mentality of the remainder of the board and their adherence to the path of least resistance, and you have one sinister concoction."

They both nodded. Together, they had nailed their synthesis.

WHAT ARE YOU THINKING?

◆◆◆

Which of the nine factors do you see at work in your organization?

Which are the most dangerous? Why?

What are you going to do about it?

Initial Report

She beat him to the office the next day, feeling relieved that it wouldn't be long before she could get back to her real work overseas. Just as he was about to saunter through the open door, humming and twirling a stir stick, she heard the ping of her inbox.

Frowning as she read the terse message, she looked up at her partner, who had stopped and was leaning against the door frame. "Orders from the Agency. They want an update – *now.*"

"What are you going to say?" he asked.

She shrugged. "I think I'll give them an overview of the trends we've uncovered. That should do it until we get things tied up. Does that work for you?"

"Sounds good."

"I'll get that out of the way right now," she said.

"Just a sec, Search. Something doesn't add up here," he said, furrowing his brow in thought. "I know that this is all pretty heavy stuff in your world, but I've been thinking – while the trends we have identified all point to poor behavior and poor judgment, is any of this really enough to bring down a board?"

Looking back up at him, she sighed. "How I wish it was. It might serve as a deterrent. From a research perspective, it really serves more as a warning and a heads-up to the Agency."

Still leaning against the door frame, he had that thoughtful look on his face that only came when he didn't trust what was going on around him. "It just doesn't seem to fit the urgency of the Agency assignment. Think about it. Calling you back all the way from overseas? Plucking me out of an active investigation? To slap a couple of nondescript folks on the hand? Does it make sense to –"

"Gov, I think about it all the time," she interrupted, clearly exasperated by the situation. "Nothing adds up." She kicked the garbage can in frustration, sending it crashing into his desk.

"So what has all this been for? To find out that the characters are boinking each other, or playing power games, or plotting silliness?" Gesturing outward helplessly with both hands, he stared at her and waited for acknowledgement.

"Don't you think I've thought of that a thousand times?" She held back the profanity she would have loved to use. "This is a low-level research study. It could have been done anytime by almost anyone. That damn Agency!" The recently replaced trash can took another beating. "What are they really up to? The only thing this does is make for some provocative reading for the governance crowd." She narrowed her eyes in suspicion. "And I can tell you this, Gov, the Agency would not be wasting its time or resources bringing you in on this unless there is an ulterior motive."

Enjoying her passion as always, he said, "That does add an extra degree of suspicion, doesn't it?"

"What could they be up to? This little soap opera we've uncovered just doesn't add up." Drumming her fingers on her desk, she squinted out into space.

He repeated his earlier question, this time slowly and with more emphasis, breaking her concentration. "Hey, Search, is it enough to bring down a board?"

Shaking her head in response, she answered. "As much as I think it should be, pragmatically it won't happen."

"Then what are we here for? And why us?" His calm musings matched her more animated approach.

Looking him straight in the eyes, she asked earnestly, "We really are missing something, aren't we, Gov?"

"Yep, and I think I know what it is. Look, could you do me a favor?"

The Agency

"They're getting close."

"Too close."

"Time to end this."

"We have what we need."

"Send them back."

Final Analysis

Later that afternoon, the Researcher was working in the office when the Detective swung open the door with a flourish. His brown eyes were flashing.

"We got them!" The glee in his voice was unmistakable.

"What? How?" Engrossed in analyzing some data, she had not heard him come in.

"Remember what we said was the only element missing for a juicy novel?"

Now he really had her attention. "You're kidding."

"Nope. Seems like our little club has overplayed their role in more than one way." He was definitely having fun.

"Ahhh, that would explain so much!"

He looked ready to burst.

She eyed him expectantly and finally asked, "Are you going to fill me in?"

"The almighty Agency is being sued – big bucks!" He was grinning from ear to ear.

Her eyes widened. "No way! They have never been sued before. Threats, of course, but nothing

I know of ever materialized." Nibbling her lower lip while anticipating a myriad of possibilities, she added, "They're not going to be able to keep this quiet for long."

"You got it. The Agency got some anonymous tip concerning negative board member behaviors and actions, with a threat of making this stuff public that apparently initiated this whole thing. The Agency is trying to find out exactly who is dirty and whether the board acted improperly, either individually or collectively. They need a scapegoat – and bad!"

Sitting back in her chair, she nodded. "That explains the immediate response I received when I emailed our status report. They wanted more specifics, right away. I was just putting the information together to zip off." Looking up at him, she asked, "By the way, where did you get this stuff?"

Plunking down into his chair, still grinning, he explained. "It was hiding right under our noses, Search. When we were joking around about writing a novel, and the essential elements required for the readers, it got me thinking about the missing element."

"The money."

"Yep. Made a few inquiries, and the info just came through. By the way, thanks for that decoy call you made to the Agency. Gave me a little cover to get what we needed." He winked in gratitude.

"Glad to help," she said, "even when I don't have a clue what's going on." Folding her arms across her chest, she looked expectedly at her partner for the rest of the story.

"Needed to keep you innocent in case things didn't go as planned."

"Gee, thanks," she said.

He kept going: "You are going to love this, Search. Found out that the auditors had uncovered some anomalies in the financial records." His voice took on an ominous tone, but the corners of his mouth were still turned up in an impertinent grin. "The proper controls, the Organization's own policies and procedures, had not been followed. There were tons of inconsistencies in the data. Apparently that was the red flag, and whoever the anonymous source is knows all of this."

Unfolding her arms and putting her hands on her hips, she let out a deep breath. "Who would have thought? That board had all of their governance angles covered in spades, going back to the work of Wilson and his board. They had the best documentation I have ever seen. Clean, clear and comprehensive."

"Seems our little club got too cocky and decided the rules weren't made for them. Kiss of death." He slowly twirled his pen between his fingers, still savoring his latest findings. "Sackmaster – and her single-minded focus of conducting the most rapid meetings in history – failed to do her due diligence, just like you said. She's totally unqualified. Such negligence might have been overlooked for a long time in any other area other than finance." His grin disappeared for a moment. "You never mess with finance."

"It all makes sense now," she said. "The minutes from the meetings, both the full board and the audit committee – or to be more accurate, the lack thereof – sure confirm what you have found."

The grin on the Detective's face returned and widened. "It gets better."

She sat straight up in her chair. "You're kidding."

"When these concerns reached the top dog at the auditor's office, things really started to move. Apparently, the head honcho was aching to bring these guys down. There'd been suspicions for the past few years that things were deteriorating within the company. The auditing staff had been treated very disrespectfully – requested information never arrived, explanations were weak and rude. That soppy VP Dung I told you about, he was covering his lack of competence with arrogance and stalling tactics, talking down and being generally uncooperative and obstinate."

After thinking for a second, she added, "The board finance committee should have caught this."

"Oh, they knew. And even supported that lousy VP Dung. Took his advice that the auditors were simply a nuisance."

"Let me guess," she said, "the finance committee was composed of our nefarious board members."

"Close. And sadly, a couple of others must have been too busy to dig into things or to deal with the issue so as to –"

"*Make no waves*," they said in unison, rolling their eyes.

The Researcher closed her eyes for a moment and then got mad, her cheeks reddening in the process. "Not again! They didn't do their darn due diligence. Not one of them!" She did not want to believe that a board could be so naive or arrogant, or maybe both. How she wished the expletives on the tip of her tongue could be released!

The Detective waited her out and then continued. "During the past few audits, the lead auditor relied on Vinn to get the information his team needed to complete their work. She was oblivious to the situation, of course, and as per the norm, she provided what was asked for without any fanfare. From the looks of things, she didn't have a clue what was boiling behind the scenes."

Darkness passed over the Researcher's face. "What a shame."

"Search, it's the jealousy factor at work once again. Apparently, she was even publically thanked for her cooperation by the lead audit guy when the audit results were presented at an open board meeting. Media were there and everything."

The Researcher sat up straight again. "Something doesn't add up. I thought you said the audit was incomplete and inaccurate."

He set his pen down and leaned back with his arms crossed behind his head. "I did. The list of problems from the auditors was longer than the financial statements, and this occurred for three years, if you can believe it."

"That's interesting. The minutes don't reflect any of this." Leaning her chin on her upright hand, she pursed her lips. "Both the president and the board chair must have known. They both sit on the finance committee." This unwanted revelation hit her, and she rubbed her forehead in exasperation. "My goodness! Add doctoring the minutes to our list of infractions."

There was an extended pause in their discussion as each absorbed the information they had shared.

WHAT ARE YOU THINKING?

♦♦♦

How seriously do you take financial reports and audit reports? Explain.

Do you take the time to thoroughly review the information? Why? Why not?

Do you question the information or ask for details, even if you are not part of the finance/audit committee? Why? Why not?

The Detective was the first to break the reverie.

"Enough to bring down a board now, Search?" His smile had disappeared; he was deadly serious.

She mirrored his expression and tone. "I would think so. All the evidence indicates they were acting collectively. It would be hard to try to pin this on one person, no matter how incompetent, because they were all involved in one way or another. Doing nothing makes a person just as guilty as if he had direct involvement. As a researcher, all I can do is provide the facts and make recommendations on governance practices. You, on the other hand, can report your findings in a much different way, can't you?" Now it was she who smiled, but hers took on a much more sinister edge.

This time he mirrored her expression. "Yep."

Not hiding her hopefulness, she asked, "Gov, is it really fraud in your estimation?"

"Getting close. Misrepresentation or deceit defines the situation. Not sure if I can go that far here. They certainly did not fulfill their role in protecting the Organization."

Shaking her head, she stated, "What were they thinking? The board just rubber-stamped what the committee brought forward. According to the minutes, there weren't any questions, and it was unanimous. Unfortunately, I'm beginning to believe that's more common than you might think. How naive could those people be?" She took a deep breath and asked, "By the way, who's suing the Agency?"

"Not sure. Think it might be someone from the inside."

"Oh?" She perked up. "Now, this sounds intriguing."

"The word is that this nefarious club used its influence to share confidential employee information." A concerned looked crossed his face. "Search, gotta tell you, this doesn't surprise me one bit. From what I heard from this dark little group, no one was immune to their disparaging comments, and no topic was off limits. It's sad that Dung was so insecure that he got drawn into it. Nice enough guy when you first meet him, but wimpy and has 'Poor Me' written all over his face and tone." He made a disgusted face to emphasize his dislike for the VP.

Pushing her hair back from her face, the weary Researcher mused, "This just gets more bizarre by the minute."

The Detective fidgeted with his eraser. "From a legal perspective, this one might be even bigger than the concerns from the auditor. The courts do not deal lightly with confidentiality issues."

Still thinking through the possibilities, the Researcher interjected dejectedly, "Let me guess, Vinn was the victim of their breach." She looked at the Detective for confirmation.

With his hands on his knees, he tilted his chair forward and replied, "That's the word on the street. They wanted to bury her good so she had no means of retaliation and no opportunity to rebuild." He paused. "Man, they're cruel. Makes you wonder how many others have been caught up in their reign of terror."

The Researcher was angry at the injustice of it all. "This is so wrong. Spreading personal information around like that and, worse, probably doctoring it, which would follow their past behavior pattern. That is a serious breach of the confidentiality that they have all sworn to uphold. From a risk-management perspective, they have put their Organization at great risk. Who's going to trust that company now? Would you want to support or get involved in any way with it now?"

WHAT ARE YOU THINKING?

◆◆◆

How is confidential employee information protected in your organization? How do you know?

Which is worse: a finance breach or HR confidentiality breach? Explain.

What would you do if you discovered one of these breaches?

"The Agency must be terrified. This hits the media in all its glory, and a lotta heads are gonna roll," the Detective said.

"It's about time." She was embarrassed that her industry would stoop so low.

"Well, Search, it looks like our list of case factors just got a little longer." His voice had returned to his typical calm drawl.

As she typed, the following items were added to their list on the large screen:

- Audit inconsistencies
- Confidentiality breaches . . .

She was about to extend their former storyline to integrate all of the factors they'd uncovered, when there was a loud knock on the door.

"Yes?" they both yelled simultaneously without turning around.

The door opened slightly, and their administrative assistant poked her head around the corner. "Sorry to disturb you, but there is an urgent message from the Agency."

Finishing Up

Back in their office, they looked at one another, stunned. This should have been a happy moment, but they were both more perplexed than excited. The Researcher was a bit pale. She ran her hand absentmindedly over the smooth dark wood of her desk.

"We must have gotten to them, Gov," she said. "They want a final report by the end of the day, and we are to end the investigation immediately. Assignment completed. That's that."

The Detective looked pensive. "That was quick. Too fast for my actions and queries to have made an impact quite yet. What do you think happened?"

"It might have been my status report." She didn't feel very confident about that. There wasn't enough in it.

"Think they'll be surprised by the final report?"

"Without a doubt. Especially your part. This is exactly what they wanted to avoid. That's pretty heavy stuff."

"From what you have told me, it's more attuned with my world than yours," he said.

"Hmmm. I'm speculating here, but you know, Gov, I may have underestimated the Agency. I let my anger for being pulled away from exciting work overseas override my better judgment. I wonder if I – not you – was actually their planned distraction. If you think about it, they would *expect* an investigative report from you, but not from the focused Researcher." Seeing the look of doubt on his face, she added, "Well, maybe not the depth to which you have uncovered the final facts. Now *that* might surprise them."

He smiled at the compliment.

"Gov, if I think about it, I was put here to ensure that what you recently found did not surface at all. I was supposed to be a distraction of sorts." Stopping for a second, she squinted and squared her jaw. "I think our crafty Agency just wanted us close enough to give it the evidence to get the perpetrators, but not so close that we got the gory details. Think about it. If they wanted a true investigation, you should have been given free rein, and I should have been your support system. After all, governance is my field of expertise, not crooks."

He couldn't help but laugh out loud at her choice of terminology.

"Seriously," she continued, folding her arms in front of her, "they put me in charge so the research would take the lead. I think they believed that my focus on research would prevent the digging you did. They know I prefer to work alone and probably thought I would sideline you as much as possible."

He couldn't help but snicker a little while tossing little pieces of Post-it notes at the wall to see if they would stick. "Search, the Agency also did their share of underestimation. If we follow your line of thought, they should never have been so arrogant as to believe that two professionals wouldn't have found some common ground from which to complete their work."

"Gov, right about now, I'd believe almost anything." She started to pick up the little, yellow missiles.

The Detective sat back in his chair, his hands behind his head. "You have to admit it was kinda fun while it lasted." He raised his eyebrows, awaiting a reply.

It was her turn to smile. "Yeah, we might have that novel after all!"

"Come on, partner, let's get this thing cleaned up and get outta here. It's our chance to escape," he said with a wink.

Conclusion

She had a stunned look on her face. "That sure ended abruptly."

The Detective leaned against the door frame of their office. "Quickest exit interview I've ever had."

"It makes me suspicious, Gov."

They both spontaneously laughed out loud.

"Well, more suspicious than even before," she tried to explain between bursts of laughter. "They sure didn't want to talk about the case, especially your final conclusions."

The Detective sobered a bit. "You know, Search, your theory looks more and more like fact. They weren't happy that we got in that far. Whew, not happy *at all.*"

Her eyes danced with delight. "Don't you just love it!"

He enjoyed her unbridled enthusiasm. The Agency could be extremely directive and stifling. "Do you think there will really be any repercussions, or am I whistling in the dark?"

"It's hard to say," she replied, some of the enjoyment dissipating. "There really should be in this case, with such severe breaches of conduct. However, the Agency has a history of sweeping these things under the carpet. It's the same story all over again. They don't want to make waves."

The Detective sat on the edge of his desk. "No wonder the board members act that way."

The Researcher tried to explain, though she really didn't want to appear like she was defending the Agency's poor behavior. "They have concerns about what it looks like to the public and would rather keep things quiet. They don't want to be put on the defensive. They really hate that."

"They may not get a choice, Search. The media are going to beat them to it. Mark my words." His tone had an ominous hint.

"That might be the best wake-up call yet."

"They have the chance to clean things up if they choose. Otherwise, they're going to be stuck with Sackmaster and her cronies for a long time. She's a loose cannon, as you know – a bad one."

Leaning back in her chair, she looked up at him. "You're so right, Gov. They have everything they need to make their decisions. The Agency histori-cally has chosen the path of least resistance. They have the opportunity to make a difference in this case. We'll see if they have the guts to do their job."

Fidgeting with his pocket change, the Detective pondered an important consideration. "Wonder if there really is this political epidemic you mentioned a while back."

She grimaced in response.

"Could be," he said, raising his eyebrows. "There doesn't seem to be much accountability built into the system."

She sat upright and said, "How I hope I'm wrong! I must say, though," – she smiled at him – "excellent observation, Detective. You sure you don't want to do this work full time? The system needs a lot of cleaning up right now. Things have gone too far for too long."

Taking a coin out of his pocket, he flipped it in the air. "Nah, think I'll leave that up to the experts. Right now corporate fraud seems way more appealing. At least if I make my case, there's a chance something will be done." Flipping the coin at her, he added, "You, on the other hand, seem to be unable to find justice."

She caught the coin in a fist, drawing a grin from her partner. "I still think of the poor staff who got hurt in all of this, and nothing will be done to compensate them in any way. Careers of innocent, hard-working people actually got destroyed by power-hungry, self-serving lowlifes. The worst part is, they have absolutely no recourse. They even get blackballed in the very system they are fighting to uphold."

He shook his head sadly. "Sometimes it feels like there's no justice, doesn't it?"

There was a long silence as both of them reflected on the recent past.

Wanting to change the subject, she finally asked, "When are you heading back to do more fraud work?"

"Right away," he said, drawling out the first word in a soothing way. "You?"

"Back to my work overseas as fast as –"

Before she could finish, the door burst open, and their breathless administrative assistant announced, to the Researcher, "Oh good, I caught you! There's an urgent call for you. It's the Agency."

They groaned and rolled their eyes in unison.

WHAT ARE YOU THINKING?

◆ ◆ ◆

What constitutes board
mismanagement?

What should be done about it?

How can you prevent it?

About the Author

Dr. Austin, an executive consultant to corporations, not-for-profits, and government agencies, has extensive and diverse board governance experience spanning the corporate, national and local levels.

Notes

Notes